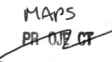

The Six Bridges of

HUMPHREY THE WHALE

by Toni Knapp

Illustrated by Craig McFarland Brown

ROBERTS RINEHART PUBLISHERS

Published in the United States of America by Roberts Rinehart Publishers, 121 Second Avenue, Niwot, Colorado 80544

Published in Great Britain, Ireland, and Europe by Roberts Rinehart Publishers, Main Street, Schull, West Cork, Republic of Ireland

Published in Canada by Key Porter Books, 70 The Esplanade, Toronto, Ontario M5E 1R2

Library of Congress Cataloging-in-Publication Data

Knapp, Toni.

   The six bridges of Humphrey the Whale / by Toni Knapp; illustrated by Craig McFarland Brown.
    p. cm.

   Summary: Describes the extraordinary journey of a young humpback whale who, during the annual migration from Alaska to Mexico, leaves his pod and swims into San Francisco Bay and, after some harrowing adventures, winds up in the Sacramento River Delta.

   ISBN 1-879373-64-5
   1. Humphrey (Whale) — Juvenile literature.   [1. Humphrey (Whale)
2. Whales.]   I. Brown, Craig McFarland, ill.   II. Title.
QL795.W5K58   1989   89-8417
599.5'1 — dc20   CIP
                                                AC

Printed in Hong Kong by Colorcorp

For Humphrey
and all the Whales
in all the oceans.
And Kevin, too.

TK

To Uri
And the Humphrey
in all of us.

CMB

Acknowledgments

We wish to thank a few very generous people who provided invaluable materials and shared their memories of Humphrey: Sally Downs of Rio Vista for her personal collection of memorabilia; Jack Findleton of Sacramento and author of *The Great Whale Rescue*, for retracing with the illustrator his memorable rescue of Humphrey; the CMMC for its final report; and marine biologist John Calambokidis for providing photographs and documented sightings of Humphrey since 1985, and detailed information verifying his unknown status since 1990; Laurie Gage, staff veterinarian for Marine World Africa USA for her first-hand account of Humphrey's 1990 dilemma; and Darryl Bush, staff photographer for Marine World Africa USA for his photo of Humphrey's stranding in 1990.

This is about Humphrey, as irrepressible and joyful a whale as the sea could hold, who listened to his own inner song, and did something no whale had ever done before. One day, he left the Pacific Ocean and went in search of adventure by swimming upstream into the fresh waters of the Sacramento River Delta, and lived to tell about it.

For twenty-six days, Humphrey toured the river and its tangled maze of shallow, dangerous inlets called sloughs. It was in one of these that he became trapped, 75 miles inland from the sea he loved, behind one of the six bridges that marked his strange odyssey.

I would like to tell you about his incredible journey. Most experts would have you believe he made a mistake when he turned left at the Golden Gate Bridge instead of swimming straight ahead with his pod. But I think they got the account wrong when they said he was confused by the tide and was probably sick. The truth is, just as many people believe he made the decision to take his now-famous detour simply because he was bored with the sameness of his life and wanted a change.

This is what he did.

Humphrey left Alaska at the appointed time in the company of thirty other Humpbacks. On a night when clouds obscured the moon and a warning chill was in the air, the whales knew it was time to go, for winter was coming soon. From Alaska, where the ocean waters are cold and wild, they swam past jagged mountains and icy fjords until the land softened and stretched beyond Canada and down to California.

All the starlit nights and autumn days he cruised joyfully south, plowing up and down through the sea at a steady 3-4 knots toward the warm, sheltered lagoons of Mexico's Baja Peninsula. There, all the whales would rest and

The Six Bridges

Golden Gate
Richmond-San Rafael
Carquinez
Benicia
Rio Vista
Liberty Island

Migration distance - Alaska to Mexico about 5000 mi.

play and calves would be born in the gentle waters. The journey had been long and hard, but already they were halfway there.

The herd kept moving at a steady pace, taking little time to rest along the way, even though Humphrey had a tendency to frolic at odd times. One glorious, sun-warmed morning, his double spouts filled the air with gossamer balloons of mist. He swam around his friends, prodding them with his long bumpy snout, but they ignored his playful overtures. He breached through the air and crashed into the waves in a thunderous explosion of whitewater. He lobtailed repeatedly and tweaked their patience with a wave of his exquisite winglike flipper, but the whales paid no attention and kept on swimming.

Friday, October 10, 1985. An eight-year old Humpback whale is sighted in San Francisco Bay.

Oct. 11-13 — Whale is tracked by scientists as he swims through San Pablo and Suisun Bays and under Richmond-San Rafael, Benicia and Carquinez Bridges, and up the Sacramento River.

To the right lay the soft ocean wilderness between California and Hawaii, where some of their Humpback friends had gone. Straight ahead waited their winter haven near the tip of Mexico. But to the left, the familiar coastline opened under a magnificent bridge that arched against the red morning sky, and stretched across a wide expanse of water.

The whales continued quietly on course, but Humphrey poked his mighty head straight up out of the water and into the sunlight. Spyhopping in a little circle, he bobbed up and down in the glittering waves like a floating rock, blue inquisitive eyes focused on the distant, mysterious sight.

His world knew no boundaries. He was as free-spirited as the winds that blew and the sea that held him. Yet, something about the bridge entranced him, and he did a very strange thing. He banked and turned abruptly left and, leaving the safety and comfort of his pod, sailed under the Golden Gate Bridge into San Francisco Bay.

Blowing and sounding happily, he plunged into the choppy, windswept waters and frolicked around the harbor islands, dodging ships, barges and noisy little boats that whistled and tooted as he glided by, and a submarine that hummed and beeped much like other Humpbacks.

Propelled by the up-and-down motion of his powerful flukes, he swam further through the bays and under three more bridges. Each one spanned the sky like steel ribbons suspended midair, rumbling overhead with deafening noises unlike any he had ever heard in the depths of the sea. But Humphrey's curiosity was stronger than his fear, and he sprinted under each one with courage.

At any time he might have reversed direction and sped back to the ocean, but that would have meant going back under the terrifying bridges. And what

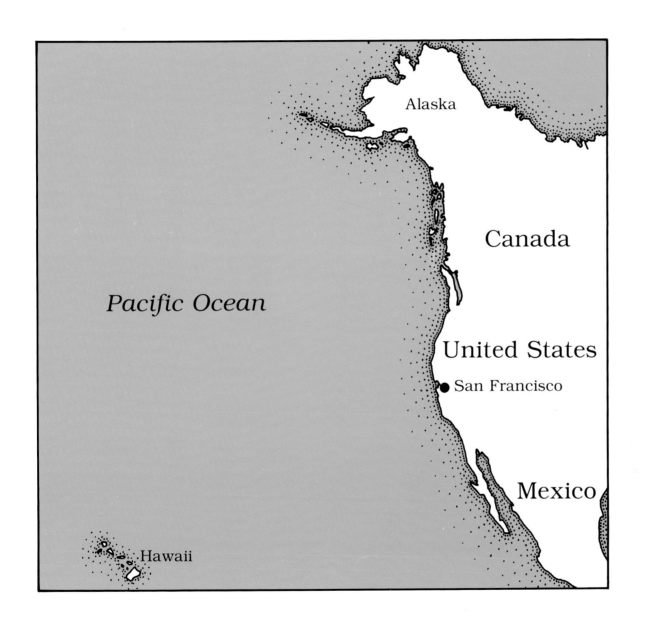

The mighty San Joaquin and Sacramento Rivers meet and merge at Suisun Bay between Collinsville and Pittsburg.

Oct. 14 — Humphrey arrives in the Rio Vista area.

might have been incomprehensible to any other whale, seemed perfectly reasonable to Humphrey. He continued to probe his new world with the zeal of an eight-year-old explorer on his solo maiden voyage away from home.

The days alternated between brilliant sun and dismal fog. But each night the hills and shores and water around him glimmered with lights as bright as the stars that guided him. He steamed along, following the sweeps and bends of the bays as they curved past waterfront towns, parks, smelly refineries, busy wharves and crowded marinas, until he came to a place where the confluence of fresh water and salt water mingled and rushed toward the ocean. His aimless meanderings had led him to a full-flowing river that felt strange on his skin and moved differently than the sea. As he swam further, Humphrey began to feel heavy and tired. Without salt in the water, he had to work harder just to keep his blowholes above the surface. But the river sang with music that whispered and sighed and gently coaxed him to follow bravely where it led.

The river was Humphrey's turning point. No one has said this before, during all the to-do about his trip, but that was where he really made his mistake. In spite of his enormous brain and great intelligence, he ignored all instinct and common sense, and continued swimming upstream like a salmon. Finally exhausted from the sheer effort of navigating through waters that wanted to sink him, he stopped to rest near a small river town in the heart of the Delta called Rio Vista.

Spouting leisurely, almost drifting in the quiet shadows, he sensed that his herd had not waited and was following the ocean highways without him. He missed their glorious singing and loving touches. For the first time in his young life, he was completely alone and very lonely. Now, deep in this salt-free inland waterway, saddened by melancholy memories of the ocean, he stretched out flush with the surface and went to sleep, his tail and flippers gently treading water. His restless night passed slowly into dawn, when his presence in the river was finally discovered.

Nothing was the same after that.

The misty light of early morning brushed softly over Humphrey's gigantic back as he floated near shore. His tell-tale spouts had given him away, and both sides of the riverbanks swarmed with alien beings. From every direction, cars honked and people shouted and called him Humphrey.

And what did he do? What Humpbacks do best — he played. Up from the depths rose a tail unlike any seen before in that or any river — black on top and white underneath, it spread 18 feet from tip to tip, battle-scarred and barnacled from a life at sea. It fanned the air like a butterfly before he surfaced to spout and dive again. His undersides were the opaque white of water-polished shells, as were the splendid flippers that extended like wings from each side. Humphrey rolled and glided in the swirling currents of jade-colored water, waving his scalloped flippers at the friendly, hysterical aliens, and spouting warm plumes of mist that could be heard miles away.

When he tired of the game, an unaccountable and powerful force surfaced from deep in his memory. He suddenly sensed it was time to leave this strange place and its odd inhabitants, and go back where he belonged, and he sped downriver in a familiar direction, unaware of the dangers that lurked ahead. He had not learned yet that the inconsistent river could be very deep here, or very shallow there, until his white belly scraped bottom, and his massive body came to a standstill, anchored in the mud and stuck by its own weight. For two terrifying hours, he lay marooned in the sun, trapped on a sandbar in alien shallows. The pressure of his unsupported weight

Oct. 15 — Two windsurfers notice a whale floating near the riverbank.

Humphrey
Length - 45 ft.
Weight - 40 tons
Body width - 10 ft.
Body height - 12 ft.
Pectoral fins - each 15 ft.
Flukes - 18 ft.
Life expectancy - 45-50 years.

Oct. 15 — Whale becomes stranded on a sandbar at Decker Island, about 6 mi. south of Rio Vista.

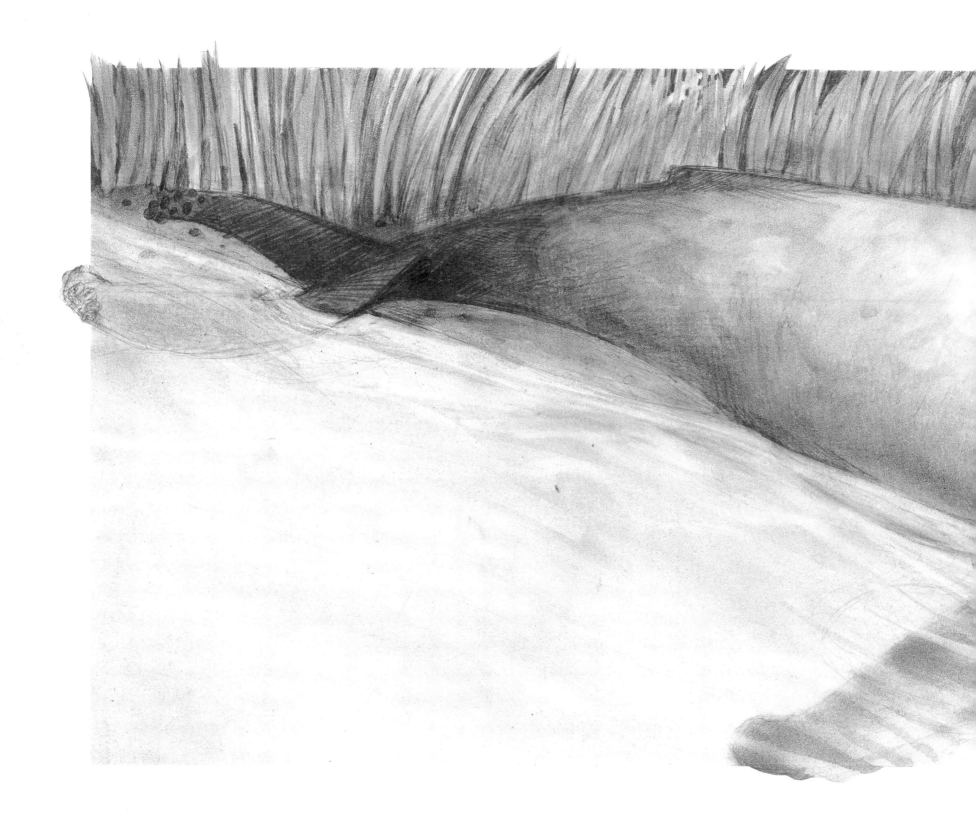

crushed against his ribs and lungs, and all his grace and beauty suddenly collapsed into a welter of flabby folds and lumps. Humphrey could not swim off, nor could he speed the pull of the moon on the tides that would float him safely away. He was afraid. He could die there, and never see his beloved ocean again.

With a sudden, frenzied thrusting of flukes and flailing of flippers, and help from the incoming tide, he thrashed and pulled and pushed until he was off the sandy prison and back in the water. At the river's edge, those who had been watching sighed and moaned with relief. But Humphrey, frantic and confused, dashed back upriver as far as the lift bridge that loomed in the distance. The low-slung Rio Vista Bridge rattled under its own weight and groaned in the wind as it spanned the width of the river. Remembering the other frightful bridges, he approached this one cautiously and swam its length several times before braving the plunge underneath.

From there, the river narrowed more and more, as Humphrey entered the land of the sloughs. He cruised around the endless islands formed by high, wide levees where uncharted waters spread into a tangled web of shallow, narrow inlets and dangerous shoals. He swam past pear and peach and walnut groves. Cattle and sheep grazed near the riverbanks and under the levees that protected them from an overflowing river. Sometimes, where the land was lower than the waterways, he swam as high as rooftops.

Oct. 15 — Humphrey swims under the Rio Vista Lift Bridge. Bridge is 270 ft. long, 20 ft. above water.

Slough — Pronounced "sloo."

Oct. 15 — CMMC begins rescue plans. Biologists play recorded sounds under water of Humpbacks and Orcas (Killer whales) to lure Humphrey out of river. He is not fooled.

Humphrey, a noble creature of the infinite sea, wandered in an absurd landscape of fruit trees and shallow creeks. Up and down he went, between the deep waters of Cache Slough and the nefarious bridge. The quiet waters and riverbanks became a circus of activity that centered on his every move. From a river that was home to all manner of fish, a 45-foot Humpback Whale had emerged, and caused quite a stir.

At the upper reaches of Cache Slough, strange things began to happen. The unmistakeable threatening voices of angry Killer Whales roared through the currents, followed by the little clicks and chirps of female Humpbacks. If he obeyed his instincts, he would run from one and follow the other, but something about the sounds made no sense and he stayed where he was until they mysteriously stopped. Humphrey was more tired than he had ever been before. His breathing was slower, and already the fresh water was taking its toll. The hideous barnacles that plagued his body with pain and misery had mercifully died and fallen off, but his glistening black skin was turning grey. He dropped from sight into a good feeding spot, and spent the night quietly in the peaceful depths of the slough, his blowholes barely visible in the moonlight.

The next day, he gracefully rolled and glided in the morning sun. Through the tall, waving marsh grass and tule that fringed the banks, his great intelligent eyes observed the crowds that had flocked to the river like migrating ducks. While he amused them with his antics, a fleet of boats determined to guide him back to sea lined up nearly the width of the waterway and headed toward him. He felt them coming. Humphrey was confused and uncertain. Did they want to play? He surfaced and splashed, but they kept coming. He spun in a whirl of foam and swam rapidly south, but the fleet followed behind, tracking his footprints on the water left by his fluke-up dives.

Oct. 16 — Sacramento Sheriff's Department attempts to herd Humphrey back to sea with a fleet of Coast Guard and pleasure boats.

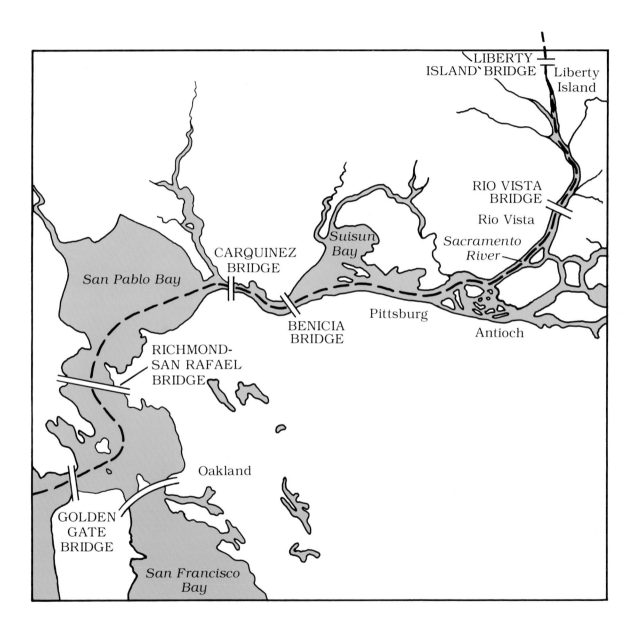

On the banks, everyone yelled and jumped up and down and cheered as Humphrey fled the posse. He sped along at three knots, not understanding why his friends were menacing him in this strange new game, but it was a good race, as he led them on a merry chase as far as the lift bridge. There he stopped.

Sandblasting machines screamed overhead, and the horn-honking snarl of traffic reverberated in the water with fearsome intensity. Trapped between the threatening bridge and the boats that kept pushing him toward it, Humphrey's gentle disposition changed from trusting to hostile. He rolled on his side and slapped the water angrily three times, first with one flipper, then the other, warning them to stay away. As the boats closed in, he raised his mighty flukes and slammed the surface with a crack of thunder and explosion of water. Then he dived and disappeared from sight, leaving only a footprint behind to mark the spot where he had been.

Upriver, he resurfaced and scooted north, skimming past rooftops and trees and a blur of sheep, spouting all the way back to Cache Slough, where feelings of sadness and confusion flowed through his great and gentle heart. He wanted only to go home to the sea.

He was left in peace for two days. The river returned to its busy ways, but the boats and barges kept a safe distance from the gentle giant in their midst. Humphrey swam undisturbed, spouting happily in Cache Slough, but the riverbanks and creaking bridge still overflowed with whalewatchers from sunrise to near darkness. Sometimes he would lift one of his majestic white flippers out of the deep water and reward them with a wave, or lobtail and spout to their delight. But mostly he did exactly as he pleased.

Oct. 17 — Scientists test sound levels under Rio Vista Bridge, and officials order all repair work stopped. Humphrey swims into Cache Slough.

When at last they went away, he floated close to the comforting shore and listened to the crickets and other mysterious rustlings of nighttime. Then he meandered to the lift bridge, wanting so much to swim past it, but his fear of it was insurmountable. Even though the ugly machine noises had stopped, it still seemed unfriendly, and Humphrey swam upstream again.

The turns of the riverbanks unfolded into even more hostile sloughs to confound him. He tried them on, as if looking for one that would fit his gargantuan size. Knowing all the while he ought to be heading in the opposite direction, he went farther and farther north, until the sixth and smallest of all the bridges blocked his way. Its narrow, cement pillars locked together like shark's teeth only ten feet apart, and were filled between with old, broken pilings and assorted trash. Not counting his flippers, he was wider than the spaces, and if he stretched his flippers straight up out of the water, they reached the bridge.

Oct. 19 — Humphrey swims under Liberty Island Bridge and into Shag Slough. Bridge is only 100 ft. long and 15 ft. above water.

Humphrey eyed the Liberty Island Bridge suspiciously as a sudden, instinctive fear shivered along his skin, warning him of an unknown but very present danger. He hesitated too long. From out of nowhere, the gunshot shattered the pastoral silence and exploded near his flukes. Propelled by a terror he had never known, he hurled himself toward the bridge through spaces not meant for the size of a whale, squeezing his body and scraping his sensitive sunburned skin.

No one ever mentions the real reason Humphrey went under that bridge. There was all sorts of speculation, of course, and when the terrible truth leaked out of the slough, there were silent, whispered denials. No one could bear to admit that someone in the Delta had tried to kill the trapped and suffering whale. To this day, the whole episode remains a black secret that hangs unspoken when stories about Humphrey are told.

Once he got past the evil bridge, he swam a mile to the stream's dead end. The water was little more than a trickle. It contained not a grain of salt, but was spiced with toxic fertilizers and pesticides flushed from the farmlands that burned his eyes and skin like flames.

Exhausted and terrified, Humphrey sank miserably to the bottom of the shabby mudhole. His friend, the river, had betrayed him. It had lured him with the music of its gentle rushing and promise of adventure. It had tricked him with its endless maze of inlets that skipped around the monstrous islands and schemed to confuse him. Finally, it had trapped him in a dead-end waterway and imprisoned him with bridges.

He was hopelessly lost, driven by currents he did not understand. The stars that had always guided him told him he should be somewhere else, but not how to get where he belonged. In the middle of the murky water, he was a spouting island, sleek and grey, hardly stirring as he finally slept, his horizons lost in the grassy borders of the muddy inlet.

The next afternoon a familiar Coast Guard cutter appeared by the bridge, and his friends resumed their vigil at the stream's edge.

Humphrey avoided the dreaded bridge and swam in small circles only a few feet from cattle and sheep grazing nearby, where the water was so shallow and narrow he struggled to stay afloat. When he stranded himself again on one of those insidious shoals, he searched deep into his memory for the will to survive. Along the shore, those who grieved under the grey, melancholy sky wiped away tears and shouted, "Push, Humphrey. Push." Using all the strength he could muster, his long pectoral fins and mighty flukes pushed and dug until he got himself off the sand. But his footprints remained imbedded in the mud, strangely out of place as if from another time or another planet.

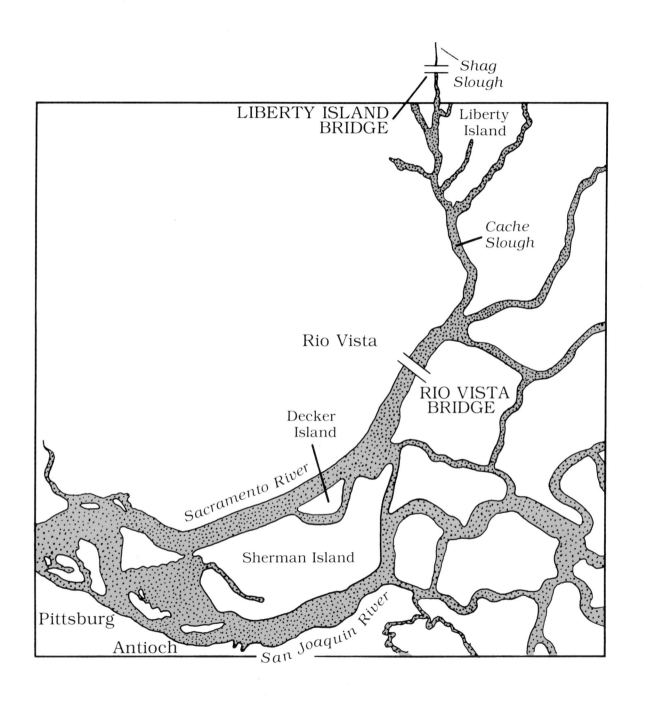

Five days passed. Humphrey lolled in the shallow waters, dappled by the sun, shrouded in fog, trapped by the bridge and watched day and night by sentries. He was hurting. Already his greying skin had formed painful blisters, and was flaking off. Breathing was painful, too. He was alone again. There were no boats to swim with — they had vanished suddenly, all at once. Even the sky was quiet. The golden October days grew shorter, and he knew by the waning light he should be somewhere else.

When things seemed at their worst, he had always managed to find a way out. He had been chased and tricked and shot at. With sheer will, he had saved himself three times from certain death in the shallows. Even in the ocean, the Orcas who long ago had attacked him and his pod were no match for his courage.

He was a Humpback Whale who belonged in the sea. Now, he floundered next to mooing cattle and 20-foot levees, with no way out. From the depths of his soul, his song poured forth into the slough, into the air, down the riverbanks, echoing in the darkness, eerie and longing and lost.

This time, he could not save himself.

Oct. 24 — Operation Whale Rescue officially begins in Rio Vista.

Oikomi: Japanese method of banging pipes underwater to create an acoustical "net."

Slough area under Liberty Island Bridge is cleared of old pilings.

Early in the morning, with the sun in hazy view, seven boats chugged single-file up the wide river, on their way to rescue Humphrey from Shag Slough. He had languished there long enough, and all the whale experts and friends who feared for his life mobilized to save him. The plan was to surround him with a special sound barrier called Oikomi, that was so loud and unpleasant he would swim under the bridge and out of the slough as fast as his tail would move him. But no one took into account the great whale's monumental stubborness.

Humphrey blew happily and rocked in the water as the boats slipped under the bridge toward his dismal swimming hole, and circled him from behind. It was a tight fit. With Humphrey's flippers extended, he was roughly the size of a basketball court emersed in a puddle. Suddenly, the dead water vibrated and blanged all around with a deafening resonance, first from one side of the slough to the other. The long, cast-iron pipes that hung from each stern clanged once each second like metronomes, pushing him to the dreaded bridge where painful memories of broken pilings and the terrifying gunshot filled his being.

Desperate to escape, Humphrey strayed into water only five feet deep, where he lay bare and exposed in the mud, grey as the weathered logs that lined the shores, under a lone, spreading, eucalyptus tree. Along the banks, his friends wiped their eyes and hung their heads in anguish, daring not to look. But within minutes, Humphrey had pushed himself back into the water where he floated and spouted weakly as the relentless pipes came at him again and again. When finally they stopped, Humphrey's plaintive cries could be heard across the distant fields, down the river, into the evening, when a barge with a giant crane appeared at the bridge. All night long, in the glow of a bright moon, Humphrey roared his pain while it whirred and cranked, dredging out

all the trash that blocked the spaces between the pillars until a way had been cleared for his exit.

Oct. 25 — Oikomi fails second time. But later, two boats persevere and push Humphrey under the Liberty Island Bridge.

When the tides and the boats came in at noon, Humphrey surprised them all with a wild, explosive rage that sent them reeling. He blew enough steam to engulf them in a cloud. Over and over he rolled, slapping the water with his powerful flippers, and slamming his flukes repeatedly in a furious display that caused the water to boil twenty feet into the air. His universe had been disturbed enough. The rescue team backed nervously away until the storm passed, while Humphrey, exhausted from his temper tantrum, sulked on the slough's muddy bottom. When eventually he surfaced, two of the remaining boats closed in and sandwiched the calmed giant between them. Humphrey felt considerably better and, like a contrite and forgiving child, he immediately nudged each boat curiously and affectionately. They seemed harmless and, comforted by their friendly, quiet closeness, he drifted into a trusting doze.

The engines roared suddenly to life. Startled out of his nap, he bolted straight ahead into the cleared openings at one end of the bridge. He thrashed and squirmed in a near-frenzy and rolled on his side as he tried to wedge himself through the cement fingers that gripped him. He pounded frantically against them until the old structure shook as though it would collapse. Dozens of people who had flattened themselves on the span so as not to disturb Humphrey's passage, hung on for dear life as they swayed above the froth.

"Push. Push!" the crowds screamed. "He's going. He's going," radioed the boats to each other. When it seemed the bridge would collapse from the struggling, it stopped shaking. There was no sign of Humphrey. The water became as still as the breathless crowd. Then, on the other side of the bridge, a smooth, perfect ring appeared on the water. His footprint.

Along the riverbanks, cheers and laughter broke the silence as he splashed and danced merrily toward Cache Slough. For three glorious hours in the autumn evening, he sailed briskly downriver as far as the Rio Vista Bridge. An hour short of sundown, before a thousand watchful eyes, Humphrey the Intrepid vanished from sight. Mud-splattered and ragged from his battle with the bridge, he rested in the tree-sheltered shadows of the riverbank, while out on the water the hunt went on. Firing parachute flares for light, the frantic flotilla swept the night-blackened waters. But Humphrey remained invisible until only a wispy fog crept along the deserted river that lapped gently against him.

The determined rescue mission resumed in the morning with renewed vigor. Before Humphrey had a chance to escape, radio transmitters were attached to his back with suction cups and the air exploded with cracker bombs shot from the boats. Terrified, he swam to the familiar shoals and deliberately beached himself again in a desperate attempt to stop the attacks. When peace was restored, he propelled himself back into the water, and went about inspecting the unfamiliar craft as though nothing had happened. He circled them all in clever figure 8's — swimming under this one, buzzing by that one, and generally having a fine time of it. In spite of all he had endured in one short day, his sense of humor was intact.

Oct. 26 — NMFS officials shoot cracker bombs — shells filled with fire cracker material and fired from an automatic shotgun — to force Humphrey under the Rio Vista Bridge.

The chase was on and Humphrey was in control. For ninety minutes, he and the boats danced a merry minuet from one end of the long bridge to the other. With every move, the ten thousand whale watchers gathered on the banks of the once-peaceful Sacramento River screamed a chorus of approval. It was wonderful. He taunted the fleet further by rolling on his side and waving a giant flipper. The crowds roared and the boats tightened formation.

Oct. 26 — Oikomi succeeds. Humphrey swims under the Rio Vista Bridge, and heads downriver.

The huge flotilla, Army ships and all, gave up the silly game, and surrounded him again with the hideous, acoustical barrier. He had no choice but to finally swim under the hated bridge and keep going, leaving it far behind as he steamed south. His faithful followers moved with him. On foot and in cars, they kept pace with his downriver migration.

All the next day he was trailed by Army, Navy and Coast Guard ships and the old, familiar boats, fifteen miles as the whale swims. Short-wave radios echoed up and down the channel, "He's ripping. He's going," and by nightfall he was finally out of the river and left to rest near the fringes of the bay, with four bridges left to go.

Oct. 27—Whale boats herd Humphrey from Decker Island to the Pittsburg area, where he frolics and performs for cheering crowds.

His wilderness home seemed only the fragment of a long-forgotten dream, yet Humphrey knew the ocean was not far away. He could feel its presence, even though after three weeks in the Delta's confining sloughs, he could hardly distinguish north from south.

Oct. 28 — Humphrey makes U-turn 4 mi. back to Decker Island. NMFS stops all rescue operations.

Following the tide, he meandered randomly upwater through the night, as was his habit, and by morning he had surfaced back in the river near Decker Island. Naturally, you can imagine that leaders of Operation Whale Rescue were not pleased by his latest backward trek. They simply could not continue going in circles, tracking his unpredictable nocturnal wanderings. Time and

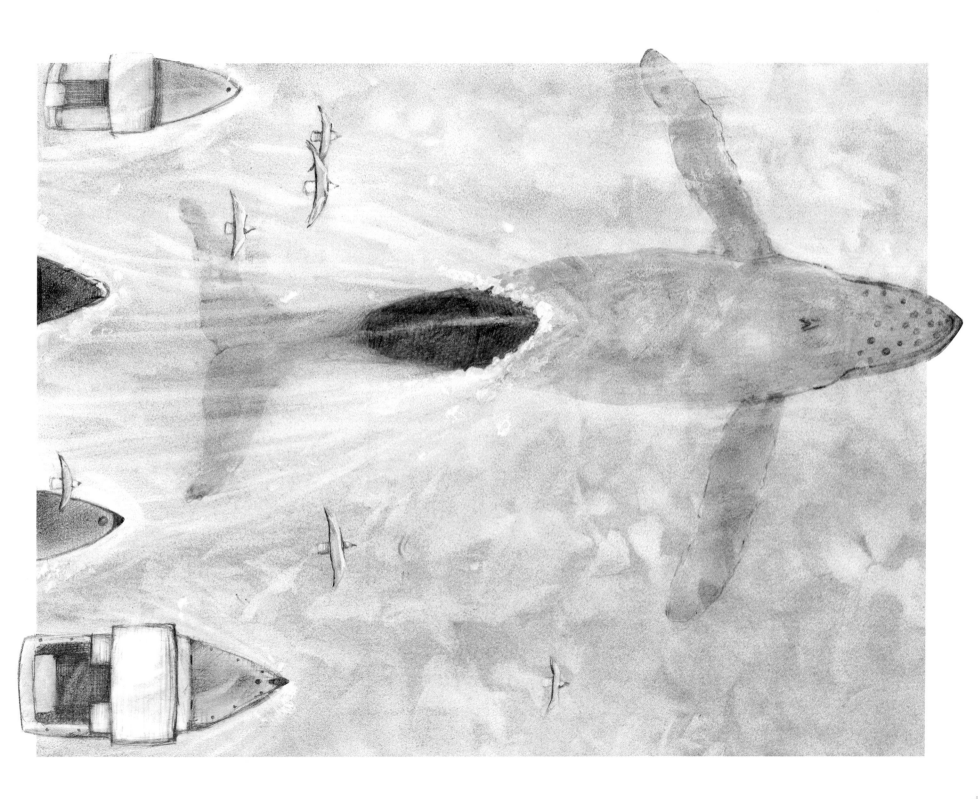

money were running out, and everyone was depressed. "The whale needs a rest," someone said. "And if he's not tired, this whole operation is."

Oct. 28-30 — All rescue attempts are suspended.

Humphrey had finally worn them out. The pipes were silenced, the boats withdrew, and the river was his. He spent his lonely days exploring its infinite tributaries, feeling their power as they poured like fountains into the bays that carried them to the ocean. Then one night, as if according to some mysterious plan, Humphrey listened to his own inner song. Fueled by a powerful instinct to follow its urgent rushings, he moved south with the river and came to rest back in Pittsburg and the bay.

Oct. 31 — Humphrey moves south on his own to Pittsburg and Antioch, at the mouth of the San Joaquin Rivers. Operation Whale Rescue resumes.

The evening was very warm, one of early November's last struggles to hang on to fall. In the soft, muted light of sunset, Humphrey recognized one of his favorite boats bobbing gently offshore. He swam toward it, rising higher in the water than usual so that his head and back were clearly exposed. He circled closely, and cast an inquiring and sympathetic eye toward the despairing men on deck who, he understood with a mystic certainty, were there to keep watch over him. His simple gesture of kinship lasted only a moment before he swung away and vanished, but it was enough to revive the rescue operation.

In the warm, morning light, entire fleets filled the river from shore to shore. Army, Navy and Coast Guard ships, bigger than the great whale, floated in V formation, dwarfing the little boats on duty with the dreaded pipes. They had come for him after all, and brought the whales with them, or so it seemed to Humphrey.

The water shuddered with the long-forgotten sounds of Humpbacks feeding and came alive with their singing. He listened, entranced by the trills

Sunday, November 3 — Humphrey follows the recorded sounds of feeding Humpbacks, played from a cruiser, from Antioch past the Richmond-San Rafael Bridge to Angel Island.

and baying and mooing that awakened memories and thrilled his heart. They were coming from the huge cruiser out in front of the fleet. He lunged towards the sounds, and followed them behind the boat's smooth wake. Its speed was an easy match for Humphrey, as he began to race along side, keeping up with the flotilla's odd, meandering pattern the way he used to when sailing with his pod.

Hour after joyful hour, he danced to the music of the rivergoing Pied Piper for 58 non-stop miles, passing all the familiar landmarks of his long-ago entrance into this unknown world, and finally into windswept San Pablo Bay.

Daylight faded into darkness, but the convoy stayed with him all the way to the sky-spanning Richmond Bridge. There, the fleet retreated. The songs of the whales stopped, too, but Humphrey hardly noticed. So jubilant was he to be back in the buoyant and blissful salt water, he blew and sounded under the lights of the pier and the orange moon, floated effortlessly, glided dreamily, and frolicked the night away.

Humphrey greeted the morning with a joyous leap, flinging himself straight out of the water so that his entire length was airborne. Then backward he flew with majestic flippers spread and curved gently upward, like alabaster wings reaching for the sky, until he crashed with explosive force into the bay. He felt like a whale again! He rolled and dived and wallowed. Below the surface he hung motionless, enraptured by the sounds of his own warbling, before leaping out again. Above him, the endless steel span glinted pink in the sun, and roared with traffic, but this time he was not afraid. He knew he would never come this way again.

When the armada came for him, he led them in a final merry, zigzagging tour of San Francisco Bay. The pageant of ships followed his mischievous snake-like course as he performed for the multitudes that came to watch. With effortless power, he fanned his enormous, beautiful tail from side to side above the water. His size and cheerfulness were things to behold as he leaped and dived and waved his giant flippers, or spouted silvery mists within a few feet of the crowds. Docks and piers groaned under the weight of thousands of people who stood in the chill fog to celebrate his freedom with him.

It was time to go. All his instincts drove him forward as he picked up speed, plunging through the waves at 6-7 knots. A full gale was blowing. Sharp spray stung his skin and gusts whistled past his blowholes as he swam joyfully west. Ahead, the Golden Gate Bridge arched into fog as thick as oatmeal and, in a clear, crystallized moment, Humphrey knew where he must go . . . back to the infinite ocean and the whales, back to 10,000-mile migrations, back to the barnacles and Orcas. Back to freedom.

He covered the distance with extraordinary grace and speed, plowing against the raging water without pause. Higher and higher he rose, mounting the waves like a great horse with white-capped mane, and he sailed with the glorious sounds of cheers and screams filling the grey afternoon. "Goodbye, Humphrey. Happy sailing, Humphrey. We'll miss you, Humphrey." We love you.

Above him, the bridge held most of the city at its rails as it honored his courage and joyful spirit. Helicopters churned low overhead and foghorns blew, as Humphrey sailed majestically out of the bay and back to his kingdom in the sea. Beyond the bridge, he raised his glorious flukes once more, then slid deep into the water and disappeared in the dense fog, bearing a thousand secrets with him.

His strange inland odyssey was over.

Monday, November 4 — Freedom. Whale boat teams and a fleet of support vessels escort Humphrey into San Francisco Bay. At 4:28 p.m. he swims under the Golden Gate Bridge.

EPILOGUE

Out of the buoyant salt water, the sheer weight of Humphrey's massive head on the rocks pushed his lower jaw over his upper face. Water was continually bailed out of the jaw's cavity. *Photo credit: Darryl Bush, Marine World Africa USA.*

There you have it. The true account and faithful retracing of an extraordinary Humpback whale's puzzling odyssey. Humphrey survived his amazing and nearly fatal experience and is swimming — happy and healthy and well — in his Pacific Ocean home. News of his exploits circled the globe and, when he swam to freedom, the world cheered.

His rescue from the confines of the Delta was a result of the combined efforts of scientists, government agencies and volunteers, all who came to love him as their own.

It is also a testimonial to Humphrey's spirit. He defied aircraft, boats, clanging pipes, cracker bombs, bridges, the U.S. Army, Navy and Coast Guard, state and federal agencies, and more than 500 volunteers in a massive rescue effort that cost $90,000.

Since leaving San Francisco Bay, he has been sighted and identified in four consecutive years: August 16-28, 1986, Farallones Islands in the Gulf of the Farallones National Marine Sanctuary; August 21-29, 1987, Bodega Bay; in October 1-10, 1988, he surprised researchers by showing up in shallow waters of Drakes Bay and Bodega Harbor; and in August 1989, he was sighted by an Oceanic Society whalewatch near the buoy just outside San Francisco Bay.

The first three recorded sightings were made by marine biologists with the Cascadia Research Collective, Olympia, Washington, as part of their three year study of Humpback whales. The photograph of Humphrey's flukes was taken by John Calambokidis on August 16, 1986, eight miles off Pt. Reyes. The whale's unique markings and scars, or "fingerprints," matched perfectly with photos taken as far back as 1983 by researchers working northeast of Isabel Island, Mexico.

Humphrey was many things — sociable, affectionate, captivating, high-spirited and trusting. He journeyed inland into fresh water for reasons known only to him. He was a rugged individual in an alien world, an innocent gone astray, a renegade in a quest for freedom. He was, above all, a gentle hero.

EPILOGUE II

Humphrey must have left his heart in San Francisco Bay. Nearly five years to the day of his 1985 visit, Humphrey came back, and news of his return spanned the globe.

In the early morning of Monday, October 22, 1990, he was discovered beached in the mud flats near Candlestick Park. After freeing himself in the rising tide, he abruptly headed toward a bleak, windswept pair of small islands called Double Rock. There he stranded in shallow water, his massive head between two rocks, 100 yards from shore near the Candlestick parking lot. When the tide went out, Humphrey lay exposed in the mud.

Surrounded by wildlife experts and dozens of volunteers, Humphrey remained in his perilous situation for 24 hours. All the while he was kept calm, protected, and wet—the Coast Guard supplied water pumps to spray him, wet towels covered his back, saline solution was put in his eyes, and blood samples were taken from a small vein in his lower jaw and rushed to a local hospital.

Through the night, Humphrey was lovingly surrounded and watched—biologists set up camp on the two rocks, a Red Cross disaster truck dispensed coffee and donuts to volunteers, and caring crowds built bonfires on shore and kept a silent vigil. The good news: results of the blood tests showed he was free of any disease, and his liver and kidneys were healthy.

On Tuesday, October 23, the high tide rolled in at 2:30 P.M. It was time to move out. A salvage company brought in air compressors to create a cushion of bubbles under the whale. A Coast Guard diver wrapped a cargo net around Humphrey's head, and a Coast Guard cutter pulled him free. The whale, disoriented and exhausted, swam a short distance and beached again. Again the cargo net, again he was pulled free, and this time he was ready.

Accompanied by a flotilla of 11 boats, and cheering crowds of nearly 4000, Humphrey was herded back into deep water. The next day he toured the Bay one last time, swimming around his favorite haunts—the Bay Bridge, Pier 39, and Alcatraz. At 5:15P.M., escorted by a small Coast Guard fleet, Humphrey sailed into the sunset and through the Golden Gate to destinations unknown. He has not been seen since then.

During the annual counts of humpback whales off the Pacific Coast in 1991 and 1992, John Calambokidis of the Cascadia Research Collective, positively identified 482 different individuals out of an estimated population of 600. Humphrey was not among them. "Humphrey's disappearance is a mystery," he said. "It's not conclusive."

Why did Humphrey return to San Francisco Bay? Some experts theorize he is a superior whale, a kind of super-humpback, a risk taker more adventurous than others. Maybe he simply liked the attention and the scenery. Whatever the reasons, only Humphrey knows, and we are left only to imagine.

Where is he now? The mystery remains.

CHRONOLOGY OF EVENTS - October 10 - November 4, 1985

October 10 — Humphrey is first sighted in San Francisco Bay and identified by the California Marine Mammal Center (CMMC) Director of Education.

Oct. 11-13 — Whale tours three bays and three more bridges, tracked by the CMMC and Coast Guard auxiliary boat. As Humphrey is a member of an endangered species, regular contact begins with the National Marine Fisheries Service (NMFS), the federal agency responsible for all action taken on behalf of the whale.

Oct. 14 — Whale swims up the Sacramento River into the Rio Vista area by nightfall. Government helicopter observes his movements.

Oct. 15 — Whale is discovered by two windsurfers on the river. He later becomes stranded on a sand bar near Decker Island. Emergency volunteer staff is organized by CMMC to begin rescue operations. They try moving Humphrey out of the Delta by playing recorded sounds of Orcas (killer whales) underwater. The plan fails, and he swims further upriver under the Rio Vista Bridge.

Oct. 16 — Fleet of boats fails to herd Humphrey back under the Rio Vista Bridge. CMMC considers moving the whale using the Japanese Oikomi method — eight-foot long iron pipes are filled with water and hung from the sides of boats. When the pipes are hit with metal hammers, the low chiming sound underwater forms an acoustical "net" that directs the whale's swimming behavior.

Oct. 17 — Humphrey swims into Cache Slough. Experts test sound levels around the Rio Vista Bridge.

They believe the resonant quality of traffic and construction noise may be the reason Humphrey fears the bridge. Rescue team tests Oikomi pipes.

Oct. 18 — Whale vanishes from sight. Coast Guard withdraws vessels.

Oct. 19 - 23 — Humphrey is discovered in dead-end Shag Slough, trapped behind the Liberty Island Bridge. CMMC sends observation team to record whale's behavior, as the situation is now a matter of life and death.

Oct. 23 — Scientists and officials from the CMMC and NMFS meet with volunteers and State Senator at the Whale Rescue Command Center in Rio Vista to plan rescue strategy. Oikomi method will be used.

Oct. 24 — Whale rescue officially begins. Six boats equipped with pipes fail to drive Humphrey under the Liberty Island Bridge. That night, dredging equipment clears area under bridge.

Oct. 25 — Drive is stopped when Humphrey slaps water aggressively as boats approach. While meeting is held to decide further action, boat teams try Oikomi one more time, and succeed. Humphrey swims under the Liberty Island Bridge all the way to Rio Vista.

Oct. 26 — NMFS officials fire cracker bombs to frighten the whale under the Rio Vista Bridge. He strands himself on a sandbar for 30 minutes. Later, after performing for the crowds and leading the boats on a merry chase, he swims under the Rio Vista Bridge and south to Decker Island.

Oct. 27 — Humphrey is escorted to Pittsburg area by nightfall.

Oct. 28 — Humphrey reappears at Decker Island. Unhappy NMFS officials suspend all rescue operations.

Oct. 28-30 — Whale swims placidly, amusing ever-present whalewatchers.

Oct. 31 — Humphrey swims south on his own to Antioch. Decision is made to resume Operation Whale Rescue.

Nov. 3 — Humphrey follows the recorded sounds of Humpback whales played from a cruiser, with Oikomi pipes chiming behind. He is escorted all the way to the Richmond—San Rafael Bridge by a flotilla of more than 50 U.S. Army, Navy, Coast Guard and civilian boats.

Nov. 4 — At 4:28 p.m., Humphrey swims to freedom under the Golden Gate Bridge, after a last farewell performance for cheering crowds.

Helpful Definitions

Humphrey is a member of an endangered species. The Humpback is a baleen (toothless) whale of the genus Megaptera Novaengliae, which means "Big Wing of New England." The wing refers to its long pectoral fins that equal a third the length of its body.

Blowing or spouting - Warm mist, not water, expelled after each breath. Baleen whales have two nostrils at the top of the head and spout a double blow that can often be heard a mile away.

Breaching - the Humpback's ability to hurl its entire length out of the water.

Flukes - the two halves of a whale's tail.

Footprint - the smooth circle left by the flukes on the water's surface following a whale's dive.

The "Hump" - in Humpback refers to the exaggerated roll of the whale's back when starting a dive.

Pectoral fins - the long, winglike flippers that measure up to 15 ft.

Pod (or herd) - a group of whales.

Sacramento River Delta - a maze of complex waterways formed by the confluence of the Sacramento, Mokelumne and San Joaquin Rivers as they flow into San Francisco Bay. The Delta's 1000 miles of channels contain hundreds of islands made through dredging and levee-building.

Slough - "sloo" - a narrow, shallow inlet from a river.

Sounding - Before making long or deep dives called "sounding", whales prepare themselves with breathing exercises that allow them to dive 500-700 ft. for 3-30 minutes.